Confusion
Reigns

Confusion Reigns

A Quick and Easy Guide
to the
Most Easily
Mixed-Up Words

---

by James S. Harrison

Illustrations by Kimble Mead

ST. MARTIN'S PRESS • NEW YORK

Design by Jeremiah B. Lighter

Library of Congress Cataloging in Publication Data

Harrison, James S.,
    Confusion reigns.

    1. English language—Homonyms. I. Title.
PE1595.H37   1987   432'.1   87-16422
ISBN 0-312-00582-2 (pbk.)

First Edition

10 9 8 7 6 5 4 3 2 1

Introduction

The day-to-day arena of spoken and written communication has always been a perilous place, fraught with endless possibilities for embarrassing blunders by even the most wary—and I don't mean just from "blooperish" slips of the tongue. You can have a fine grasp of grammar, be a whiz at spelling and syntax, and still occasionally find yourself in a quandary about which word to use. And these days it seems that those of us who want to be precise are having a harder time than ever; there is a lot working against us.

For one thing, there is the constant bombardment of sloppy English that we are subjected to from what we hear and read; and not just what's overheard on the bus or read in a piece of graffito. I mean heard on TV or radio and read in every conceivable kind of printed matter. These are strong influences, and if we hear and see a word misused enough times, it takes on a certain "correctness." Time and time again in this book I was tempted to open a paragraph by saying, "No matter how often you see this in your favorite—very respectable—magazine or hear it on the nightly news, it just isn't correct."

Nor can we count on that old standby, the dictionary, to help us out much anymore. Not only do the murky definitions often simply add to the confusion, but most present-day editions have adopted a free-for-all, anyway-you-want-it-is-okay approach. They try to be agreeable by letting us say anything we want, but that turns out to be no help at all. Usage handbooks do provide a bit of guidance, but they too can get entangled in wordy thickets that are hard to get through—or even into.

Then, of course, there are the built-in problems of the language itself: A one- or two-letter change in spelling can change a word's meaning completely. A different suffix can make a subtle—but important—difference. Sometimes two very different words get confused because their meanings apply to things that are very similar (turtle and tortoise, for instance).

So, in an attempt to be of some assistance, I offer this book. It is an accessible little volume that provides a simple, straightforward, and amiable (see page 10) escort past 200 or so of the stickier wickets in the English language. It's not a spelling or grammar guide, but an investigation of pairs of words that, because of their closeness of spelling or meaning, are frequently mixed up. Each word is defined, an explanation of where the confusion lies is given (if it's not immediately apparent), and usage sentences offer further explication. There are lots of memory aids (aka mnemonics) throughout. Many of these may seem a touch goofy, or even inane, but in my experience, the wackier these things are, the more they help.

My hope is that this book will be a useful reference guide for self-help; an authority to settle arguments; and even the source of enlightening and entertaining word games. Most of all, I hope that it will do a bit to keep English intact, and be fun to pick up and read in the bargain.

— J.S.H.

Confusion
Reigns

Abjure/Adjure

The only thing that these near twins have in common is that both imply serious, powerful feelings.

Abjure: to renounce or reject.

Adjure: to plead with or command very strongly.

In an attempt to abjure her faith in the capitalist system, Doreen cut the credit card into ribbons.

Assuring me that it was delicious, she adjured me to try the raven's-claw aspic.

MEMORY AID: Think of **ab**jure and **ab**andon.
Think of **ad**jure and ple**ad**.

Ablution/Absolution

Both words are often used in religious contexts.
Ablution is the act of cleansing oneself.
Absolution is the pronouncement, usually by a priest
or minister, that one is forgiven one's sins.

There had been many visitors to the shrine
that afternoon, and the water was a bit murky;
we decided to forgo the ablution.
The parishioners always felt a great deal better after the absolution.

MEMORY AID: Water is **blue**, and it is used for **ablu**tions.

Acadia/Arcadia

Acadia: The early French colony in what are now the
Maritime Provinces of Canada; and/or the bayou country of Louisiana in which many of the colonists,
driven from Canada, settled in the eighteenth century.
Arcadia: A blissful pastoral region of ancient Greece
that gave its name to any pleasant, quiet spot. It's usually capitalized.

It is only a catfish's throw from New Orleans
to Acadia.
The Arcadia that many people thought they
had found in suburbia rapidly turned into
something quite different.

MEMORY AID: Think of **Ac**adia and **a Ca**jun.
Think of **Ar**cadia and the Garden of Eden, or **pa**radise.

Acclamation/Acclimation

Acclamation is an enthusiastic expression of approval made with shouts and applause.
Acclimation is the process of getting used to a new climate, environment, or situation.

There was no need for polling the delegates; they nominated Georgette for president by a thunderous acclamation.
She found that acclimation to the sudden new heights of power was not at all difficult.

MEMORY AID: Think of **accla**mation and **accla**im; **acclim**ation and **clim**ate.

3

Acronym/Anagram

An acronym is a word made up of the first letter or first few letters of other words, usually organizations or descriptive phrases (CARE: Cooperative for American Relief Everywhere; sonar: sound navigation ranging). An anagram is a word or words made up of the rearranged letters of another word or words.

When Fathers Against Raises for Teachers realized what the acronym for their organization was, they changed the name.
Spin is an anagram of *snip*.

MEMORY AID: **Acro** is Greek for top, so think of the **acro**polis on the top of a hill and remember that **acro**nyms take their letters "off the top."
4   And remember: A granma lives in Anagram.

Adapt/Adopt

To adapt is to change something to make it fit with something new.
To adopt is to choose, to take, or to accept something or someone new.

Patrice adapted quickly to the ways of his adopted country.

MEMORY AID: To ad**apt** is to become **apt**.
Ad**option** always has a sense of choice—or **option**.

Adrenalin/Adrenaline

Both are names for epinephrine, a hormone made either naturally by the body's adrenal glands or synthetically by a pharmaceutical company.

Capitalized and without the final "e," Adrenalin is the trade name for the stuff sold at your local pharmacy. Lowercased and with the "e," adrenaline is the secretion your body produces, particularly when you're frightened or excited.

My doctor prescribed Adrenalin for my bronchial condition.

Grandfather could never have leaped over the fence like that if it hadn't been for the adrenaline that suddenly surged through his system.

MEMORY AID: If you pay, you get a capital "A," but for free, you get an "e."

5

Adverse/Averse

Adverse means hostile or detrimental.
Averse means opposed to or reluctant.

The adverse publicity did not hurt Henrietta's career one bit.

Because of the hostility of the crowd, she was averse to performing in Madison Square Garden.

MEMORY AID: Remember adverse and adversity; averse and aversion.

Affect/Effect

6 One of the classic troublemaking twosomes, this is a pair that many people always have to think about in order to get right. The first thing to remember is that when you want a noun meaning result or outcome, the word is effect (affect is seldom heard as a noun). As verbs: affect means to have an influence upon, to change; effect means to bring about, to create.

All that running and other exercise finally had an effect—she died.

Her death will affect many people.

It's not often that someone can effect such an overnight transformation in people's habits.

MEMORY AID: Think of affect and alter; effect and execute.

Aid/Aide

Aid: help or assistance.
Aide: a person who gives help or assistance.

If Amanda pulls that trick many more times,
no one will come to her aid.
This time she was lucky: the president sent
one of his most efficient aides.

MEMORY AID: Remember that aides are people.

LIGHTING THE WAY

Candelabra or *candelabrum*? Not only are Latin endings perplexing to many people, but the multiple branches on a single one of these candle-holders add to the plural/singular mystery. Two or more of these elegant objects are candelabra; just one, no matter how many branches it has, is a candelabrum. (And notice that even though they hold cand*les*, they are cand*la*bra.)
Memory aid: In Latin, words that end in "um,"
      Almost rhyme and mean "one."

7

PERENNIAL SLIPUPS I

Advice and *advise*. *Advice* is the noun (always), and means a suggestion; words of guidance. *Advise* is the verb (always), meaning to recommend a course of action; to suggest. Memory aid: Think of the pronunciation of advise ("advize") and remember that you can "verbize" almost any word by adding "ize" to it (memorize, categorize, finalize).

Allude/Elude

To <u>allude</u> is to refer to something casually or indirectly.

To <u>elude</u> is to avoid or get away from something or somebody.

"You must start behaving more like a grown-up," Alvino said, alluding to the fact that I was wearing a large picture hat with lights around the brim.

By leaping inelegantly over the boxwood hedge, we successfully eluded the boorish couple we had met on the train.

MEMORY AID: Remember that an **allusion** is a refer**ral**.

8

Allusion/Illusion

An <u>allusion</u> is an indirect reference to something.
An <u>illusion</u> is a false or misleading perception.

The word "infamy" in the speech to the trade group was an allusion to the Japanese attack on Pearl Harbor.
I had the illusion that I could almost reach out and touch the rising sun.

MEMORY AID: Think of **alluding** as subtly **calling** attention to.

Alternate/Alternative

<u>Alternate</u> describes something happening back and forth; first one thing, then the other.
<u>Alternative</u> implies that there is a choice involved.

9

Alice and Harriet worked on the tunnel on alternate nights.
The alternative plan was to remain in the dungeon.

CHOICE OF SEASONINGS

Even though they both are often combined in the preparation of a single dish, an *herb* is one thing, a *spice* another. Herbs are the leaves—and sometimes stems—of herbaceous (nonwoody) plants, and are nearly always green. Spices come from a variety of growing things, but they are nearly always seeds, husks, or bark; they can be any color.

Amiable/Amicable

These friendly fellows are close in meaning, but there are discrete—and discreet—differences.
<u>Amiable</u> connotes cheerfulness and fun.
<u>Amicable</u> connotes cooperation and goodwill; the wish not to get into an argument.

The rain didn't dampen the amiable spirits of the guests at our backyard picnic.
We worked out an amicable agreement with the neighbors about the noise.

MEMORY AID: **America** has an **amicable** relationship with **Canada**.

10

CRUSHING MIXTURE

While a *mortar* isn't much good without a *pestle*, and vice versa, together they are useful in the kitchen for grinding or pulverizing herbs, spices, and other recipe ingredients. But some folks say mortar when they mean pestle, and vice versa. The mortar is the bowl into which you put the spice, herb, or whatever, and the pestle is the cudgellike thing with which you bash away.

Amused/Bemused

To be <u>amused</u> is to be pleasantly entertained or diverted.
To be <u>bemused</u> is to be perplexed, confused, or lost in thought.

We were greatly amused by the antics of the animals.
We were quite bemused when for no apparent reason the creatures suddenly ran and hid.

MEMORY AID: **Be**mused comes from a large, somewhat **mu**ddled family that includes bewildered, befuddled, and baffled.

11

Appraise/Apprise

To <u>appraise</u> is to evaluate the quality of, to judge the worth of.

To <u>apprise</u> is to notify, to inform.

A panel of experts was chosen to appraise the value of teaching pig Latin in public schools.

I am going to apprise these people of my opinion.

MEMORY AID: Always hope your appraiser praises. Hope your appriser advises.

ONE HUMP OR TWO?

12

There are two species of camel—*Bactrian* and *dromedary*. The Bactrian camel—capitalized because it's named after Bactria, an ancient Asian country—is the two-humped kind and is found in central Asia. The dromedary, found in northern Africa, has one hump. Memory aid: Instead of saying Bactrian, say "bac*two*-ian."

Avenge/Revenge

There is a subtle but distinct difference here.

Avenge connotes the meting out of punishment for a justifiable reason, or when vindicating wrongs against another.

Revenge, while perhaps sweet, has a bit of a nasty connotation; the punishment is usually to settle a score when a person sees himself as personally wronged.

Roy sought to avenge his brother's death by relentlessly hunting down the murderer.
By setting fire to the gym, Sally got revenge for not having been chosen for the basketball team.

MEMORY AID: Remember that **rev**enge can have **rev**erse results.

Bathos/Pathos

These two are alike only in that bathos might be thought of as simulated pathos.

Bathos refers to something ridiculously melodramatic, commonplace, or mawkish, particularly when one is striving for a much more exalted effect.

Pathos refers to something that genuinely evokes pity or sorrow.

The actress's big scene—when all that was at stake was a torn fingernail—was a masterpiece of bathos.

The opera, with its wonderful music and heartbreaking story, is a work of great pathos.

MEMORY AID: Bathos is often seen in B-movies.

Beside/Besides

Beside means "by the side of" (physically).
Besides means "in addition to" or "moreover."

A small vase of dispirited daisies stood beside my plate.

Besides, I wasn't in the mood for English cooking.

MEMORY AID: Since "besides" sounds plural, think of it as meaning "more."

Bi- /Semi-

Bi- is a prefix meaning two, twice.

Semi- is a prefix meaning half, or halved.

These common word-openers tend to get confused, understandably, in the constructions biweekly/semi-weekly and bimonthly/semimonthly. Bi-, in this sense, means "happening every two" (or every other); semi- means happening twice in a given period at regular intervals (twice a month, twice a year, etc.). To add to the confusion, biannual and semiannual both mean the same thing: twice a year. For something that happens every two years, the word is biennial.

It takes so long to get the artworks collected that the museum can hold a major exhibition only on a biennial basis.

Many different types of birds rest here during their semiannual migration.

15

MEMORY AID: You must **bi**de your time for the next **bi**-anything, but a **semi**-something can seem like an epi**demi**c.

Bloc/Block

A bloc is an alliance of people, nations, or factions acting together in a common interest.

A block is a largish chunk of something, or an obstacle.

Egypt, New Guinea, and Puerto Rico voted as a bloc at the gathering of nations.

They made a desperate attempt to block the takeover by the developed nations.

MEMORY AID: Think of bloc and OPEC.

Boor/Bore

16

A boor is a rude, ill-mannered person.

A bore is a person or thing that is dull and uninteresting.

Waldo is a boor. For one thing, he's always chewing gum in my ear.

Ampara, with her constant prattle about nothing but herself, is really a bore.

MEMORY AID: The "oo" in boor rhymes with the "u" in rude.

A bore might make one snore.

GENDER DISORIENTATION I

The names *Marian* and *Marion* are pronounced alike, but the former is usually the name of a female, the latter usually that of a male. Memory aid: You'll remember the female version if you keep in mind that women's names end in "a"—Maria, for instance.

Bridal/Bridle

Bridal is an adjective and means having to do with brides and weddings.

Bridle, as a noun, is part of a horse's harness; as a verb, it means to take scornful offense.

It was a very pretty midair wedding; all the members of the bridal party wore matching parachutes.

The white bridle contrasted nicely with the animal's dark hide.

Always a headstrong person, Francine would bridle at even the most practical piece of advice.

MEMORY AID: Think of **bridle** and **girdle,** both restraining devices.

17

Bring/Take

Generally, bring is used for movement to the vicinity of the writer or speaker, or to the vicinity of a person being addressed.

Take is used when the movement is away from the speaker or writer or to a third location altogether.

SHE (*thinking*): I guess I'll take the inflatable sofa with me tomorrow.

SHE (*on phone*): . . . and I'm bringing the inflatable sofa.

HE (*replying*): Oh, good. We can take it with us to the outdoor concert.

BOTH (*at concert*): We forgot to bring the sofa!

MEMORY AID: Think of "bring here" and "take away."

Bullion/Bouillon

Bullion is gold or silver in bar form.
Bouillon is broth made from meat and/or vegetables.

The gold bullion piled on the table gleamed
like a dream castle.
In the crisp air of the French countryside, the
kitchen-fresh bouillon tasted delicious.

MEMORY AID: When the word is pronounced properly,
one can hear the "ou" of soup in the first syllable of
bouillon.

Calvary/Cavalry

Calvary, capitalized, is the name of the place in or
near Jerusalem where Christ was crucified. Lowercased, calvary is a replica of the Crucifixion.
The cavalry is the part of an army that rides on
horses or, in today's armed forces, in fast-moving,
highly maneuverable vehicles.

The precise location of Calvary has been a subject of debate for centuries.
Mounted policemen are a sort of urban
cavalry.

MEMORY AID: Think of Calvary; Christ and Lord.
Relate cavalry with cavalcade and cavalier, two other
words that are associated with horses.

Canapé/Hors d'Oeuvre

Both are little nibbly things, but:
Canapés are always served on toast, crackers, or small pieces of bread.
Hors d'oeuvres (olives, marinated vegetables, sliced salami, etc.) usually appear by themselves.

The sandwiches we got on the plane were so small they might as well have been canapés. The curried almonds, stuffed mushroom caps, and other hors d'oeuvres were so good I was certain the meal that was to follow was going to be sensational.

MEMORY AID: Canapé derives from "canopy," so think of the little pieces of meat, fish, cheese, or whatever as canopies over little bread beds.

Canvas/Canvass

Canvas, a noun, is a heavy, closely woven fabric.
Canvass, either a noun or a verb, refers to the process
of personally going around to survey people, drum up
support, etc.

We were certainly lucky that the canvas was
waterproof.
Young people will canvass the entire city,
seeking signatures on a petition to ban the
uranium plant in Central Park.

MEMORY AID: By canvassing you can assay public
opinion.

Capital/Capitol

Capital: money, chief city, the top of a pillar.
Capitol: the building where a legislature convenes.
Most people have no trouble remembering that the word for invested money is capital. The confusion comes when trying to decide whether to use the a word or the o word when referring to the city. The thing to remember is that capitol is used only for a building, never a city.

We went to Des Moines, the state capital.
We visited the art museum, a printing plant, and the capitol, where we met our district representative.

MEMORY AID: Capitols have domes.

GEOGRAPHICA CONFUSICA I

Granada is an intriguing old city in southern Spain. The little island—and former British colony—in the West Indies is *Grenada* (pronounced with a long "a"—Gre-nay-da). Memory aid: To remember the spelling, think of Spanish Granada and English Grenada.

Careen/Career

Careen means to swerve and lurch, not necessarily with great speed.
Career means to move at great speed. (Stagecoaches in western movies do a lot of careening, but cars career down highways.)

Aunt Ethel, careening around the corner on her motorcycle, was a sight to remember.
The dog, joining in the fun, careered after her.

MEMORY AID: The careening teen swerved and leaned. The careering spear caused fear.

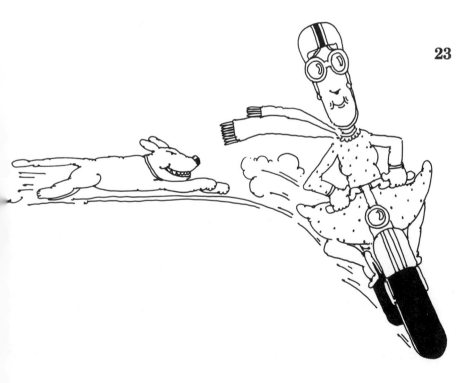

Censer/Censor/Censure

A censer is the incense burner carried by a priest during a religious service.

Censor, as a verb, means to remove parts of books, plays, documents, etc., because they are politically dangerous or morally offensive. As a noun, the censor is the person who does the censoring.

To censure is to condemn, disapprove of, reprimand.

The bishop swung the censer wildly above the heads of the throng.

It was a shame that the censor cut out Henrietta's only line in the movie.

It wasn't the first time that Congress had to censure one of its members for outrageous behavior.

MEMORY AID: Since a censer has to do with the sense of smell, think of it as a senser.

Since they both cut, think of cen**sors** and scis**sors**.

Chafe/Chaff

Chafe means to feel soreness or irritation caused by constant or repeated friction.

Chaff means to tease in a pleasant way; it is also the husk of a grain kernel.

He rubbed his hands together in anticipation for so long that the skin began to chafe.

So lacking in humor is he that it is difficult to chaff him for his foibles.

MEMORY AID: Think of ch**aff** and l**aff.**

Champ/Chomp

Both mean to chew or to munch, but <u>champ</u> is the more proper word; <u>chomp</u> is slangier, more "country"-sounding. One often hears the phrase "champ at the bit," meaning to be eager to get on with the action.

Always enthusiastic about swimming, Max began to champ at the bit the minute he saw the ocean.

Clem began to chomp contentedly on an ear of corn.

MEMORY AID: Since a racehorse "champs at the bit" in the starting stall, which is where the expression comes from, think of animals champing.

Childish/Childlike

Childish means appropriate for a child; it is usually applied to adults to describe unseemly, immature behavior.
Childlike describes ingenuous or other behavior that is like that of a child.

It may be childish of me, but I enjoy wearing the hat with the doggy ears.
There was a childlike fearlessness about Aunt Ethel as she climbed onto the motorcycle.

Chord/Cord

A chord is a combination of musical notes played together; the word can also mean a particular reaction or emotion.
A cord is a long, thin ropelike strand, including the ones in our throats that allow us to speak. Perhaps because of the musical qualities of the human voice, an "h" sometimes sneaks into "vocal cords." And perhaps because a cord can bind people together, the "h" often gets dropped from such expressions as "a common chord."

The speaker played the audience as though it were a mighty organ, hitting many popular chords.
Later, at the party, his vocal cords gave out.

Circumscribed/Circumspect

Circumscribed means to be limited by definite boundaries.
Circumspect means to be very cautious and wary in making a decision.

Because of her attachment to the beast, Farrah's life was very circumscribed.
She was so circumspect that the light had turned back to red before she felt it safe to proceed.

MEMORY AID: Think of in**scrib**ing a line and circum**scribe**.
Think of circum**spect** and su**spect**.

Cite/Site

Cite is a verb that means to quote, to call upon, to refer to.
Site, most often a noun, means a specific location—as for a building, an event, etc.

An astonished Miss Wimple asked me to cite the sources of my information.
I did her one better; I lead her to the still—smoldering site of the action.

MEMORY AID: Think of **cite** and its kin, **citation**.
A building **sits** on a **site**.

Clamber/Clamor

It's possible to do both at the same time, but:
Clamber means to climb with difficulty or awkwardly.
Clamor means to make a lot of noise; as a noun, it means a loud noise.

We were forced to clamber over the jagged rocks as the liquid oozed down the gulch.
The primitive birds overhead began a mighty clamor.

MEMORY AID: Think of **clamb**er and **climb**er and **scramb**ler.

Classic/Classical

Classic describes the best or most typical example of something (often referring to clothes, movies, literature, etc.).

Classical refers to the traditional or generally accepted standard; it is also used to describe serious music, specifically that of the late eighteenth and early nineteenth centuries. In the arts, classical style is characterized by regularity and balance.

From the thrust of her chin to the forcefulness of her stride, Miss Allwether appeared to be the classic teacher of English.

The classical rules of grammar still relentlessly eluded Amy.

MEMORY AID: "The Marriage of Figaro" is a classical music classic.

Climacteric/Climactic/Climatic

Climacteric, a noun, is a milestone or turning point in one's life, specifically menopause.

Climactic is an adjective having to do with climaxes (the kind movies and books have).

Climatic is an adjective having to do with climate, or the weather.

Men may not have any physical changes, but they often go through a climacteric just as women do.

The climactic moment came when the last helicopter finally lifted off.

My pet badger is very sensitive to small changes in climatic conditions.

Complacent/Complaisant

Complacent means self-satisfied; smug about one's situation.

Complaisant means amiable; willing (and able) to please others.

In spite of what was obviously happening to their children, the suburban mothers remained maddeningly complacent.

After a hard day at the office, Beryl was always glad to get home to her complaisant pets.

MEMORY AID: People get com**plac**ent about their **place** in life.

Complement/Compliment

Complement: something that balances, offsets, or completes.
Compliment: a bit of praise. And something that is "on the house" is complimentary.

The stark white candles were a nice complement to the deep red blossoms in the bowl.
It was easy to compliment the hostess on the table decorations.

MEMORY AID: Sometimes you might have to lie a bit to pay a compliment. And think of being **pli**ed with com **pli**mentary drinks.

Connote/Denote

This easily (and often) mixed-up close couple is a favorite of grammar-test makers. Both words are alike in that each of them has to do with getting a meaning across, but one communicates indirectly, the other directly.

To connote (the indirect one) is to imply, to suggest, to allude.

To denote is actually to indicate, to designate, to mean.

The phrase "white tie and tails" will always connote evenings on the town, elegant dancing, urbane conversation.

The airplane symbol on the city map is used to denote the location of an airport.

32

Console/Consul/Council/Counsel

A console is a piece of furniture.

As a verb, to console is to comfort or soothe distress.

A consul is a government official, usually one who looks after his country's affairs in a foreign land.

Almost always a noun, council means an elected or appointed group that governs, legislates, administrates, etc. It is made up of councilors.

Counsel, as a noun, is advice, often of a legal or professional nature. As a verb, it means to advise. The person who advises—for instance, a lawyer—is either a counsel or a counselor.

A console table usually has just two legs and is made to be set against and supported by a wall.

A bitter disagreement broke out between the two nations, and the consul was called home.

After the rash of skyscraper collapses, the city council met in an unusual weekend session.
Very clever about human relationships, Gerry is a good person to talk to when I need counsel in my personal affairs.

Contemptible/Contemptuous

Contemptible means acting in a way that elicits contempt.
Contemptuous means showing and feeling contempt.

I find their fraudulent nihilism and their arrogant self-importance utterly contemptible.
With their sneers and their swaggers, they seem contemptuous of everyone and everything.

Corespondent/Correspondent

A corespondent is the person charged with having committed adultery with the defendant (aka the respondent) in a divorce. In other words, A is divorcing B, and A might accuse B of having slept with C, and therefore also brings suit against C. C is the corespondent.
A correspondent is someone you have intercourse with by mail—or a person on TV or in the newspaper who reports from some far-off place.

Being named corespondent in the juicy divorce case gave Henrietta's career the biggest boost it had had in years.
I enjoy having him as a correspondent, but I never want to see him again in person.

Credible/Creditable

Credible means capable of being believed.
Creditable means good enough to be worthy of praise or belief.

The fact that it was raining gave me a credible excuse for being late.
Dorothy may never win a prize, but she plays a creditable game.

MEMORY AID: Think of the unbelievable opposite of credible—incredible, a much more popular word. You should never be ashamed of taking credit for something creditable.

34

Crevasse/Crevice

A crevasse is a wide, deep fissure, usually in a snow-field or glacier.
A crevice is a narrow cracklike opening in stone, plaster, etc.

I slowly moved my skis back from the edge of the crevasse.

The crevice in the wall was so small it was almost imperceptible.

Decry/Descry

To <u>decry</u> is to disparage; to strongly disapprove of with the intention of discrediting.

To <u>descry</u> means to discover or observe, particularly when the discovered thing is far away or difficult to see.

Some politicians use "the threat of communism" to decry any policy or point of view they don't approve of.

I think the senator feels that he could descry a communist on the surface of the moon with his naked eye.

MEMORY AID: When you de**cry** you often **cry** out. When you des**cry** you might say that you **spy.**

Delusion/Illusion

A _delusion_ is an incorrect belief—sometimes to the point of madness—about oneself or one's surroundings.

An _illusion_ is a deception or misleading perception.

Swaying slowly back and forth in her rocking chair, Aunt Ethel was under the delusion that she was on a horse.

A trained ventriloquist, she could create the illusion that the dog was speaking.

MEMORY AID: Remember that a **de**lusion can be slightly **de**mented.

36

Desert/Dessert

A large area of barren land is a <u>desert</u>.
The sweet course at the end of a meal is <u>dessert</u>.

The temperature, the dust, and the animals crawling about made Trent's room seem like a small desert.

It was one of those trendy restaurants where the main courses were mediocre but the desserts were excellent.

MEMORY AID: Think of **des**ert and **des**olate.
Think of the two "s's" in de**ss**ert as standing for **s**weet and **s**ugary.

Diagnosis/Prognosis

A diagnosis is the investigation, analysis, or conclusion that is made about a disease or other condition.

A prognosis is the prediction concerning how a patient will be affected—or not affected—by a disease or other condition.

The doctor made a hasty diagnosis based on only one lab report.

The always cheerful nurse made a prognosis of total recovery.

Disassemble/Dissemble

38 Disassemble means to take something apart.

Dissemble means to conceal or disguise facts or feelings.

My new mechanical gopher is easy to disassemble.

Sometimes, when the truth would do more harm than good, it is wise to dissemble.

MEMORY AID: Your dis**sembl**ing may re**sembl**e reality.

Discomfit/Discomfort

These two look and sound like they should have similar meanings, but they are actually quite far apart. Discomfit is somewhat like discombobulate; it means to thwart, to frustrate, or to throw into confusion. Discomfort means lack of comfort.

Our security measures managed to discomfit the nocturnal attackers.

The more annoyance and discomfort I can cause them, the happier I will be.

Disinterested/Uninterested

Disinterested means to be neutral and unbiased about a given situation; to have no prejudice or opinion about a given subject.
Uninterested means to be totally lacking in curiosity or concern about a given subject or situation.

Since all the witnesses had a family member involved in the incident, it was impossible to get a disinterested interpretation of what actually went on.
Celeste is uninterested in farming.

Distinct/Distinctive

Distinct means to be clearly visible or understood.
Distinctive means special, unusual.

Cosette's tattoo was quite distinct that day.
There is something distinctive about Cosette.

Distracted/Distrait/Distraught

Each member of this out-of-sorts trio has to do with being upset, or at least a bit out of it; but each word expresses a different degree of disturbance.

To be distrait, the mildest of the three conditions, is to be absentminded; a bit preoccupied.

To be distracted is to be worried or confused by problems or events.

To be distraught is to be in a state of severe mental anguish; overwhelmed by grief, worry, etc.

The wedding music was boring, and the organist grew quite distrait as she played.

First the caterer walked off the job, then it began to rain; the mother of the bride became so distracted that she began to pace.

After reading the note from the groom's best friend, the bride became so distraught that she had to be given a sedative.

41

MEMORY AID: To keep the extremes here in mind, remember that distrait is pronounced "distray," so think of straying thoughts.

And remember that distraught rhymes with overwrought.

UNLIKELY BEDFELLOWS II

Diplomat and *diplomate*. A *diplomat* is a person who is good at diplomacy or whose job is in that field. A *diplomate* can be anyone who holds a diploma, but it usually refers to a medical doctor who has earned a certificate for rigorous work in a particular field of his profession.

Memory aid: Think of diplom*ate* and certific*ate*.

Downstage/Upstage

<u>Downstage</u> refers to the stage area closest to the audience.

<u>Upstage</u> refers to the area farthest from the audience. As a verb, "to upstage" means literally to force an actor to deliver his lines facing away from the audience.

On opening night the dog trotted downstage and began snarling at a fur hat in the front row.

"Upstage me once more and we're finished," screamed Henrietta to her husband of twenty-four hours.

MEMORY AID: In early theaters (and occasionally today) the stage was raked (slanted) to give the audience a better view, so actors literally moved up the stage and down the stage.

Earthly/Earthy

Earthly applies to things found on and originating from the planet Earth—as opposed to things heavenly, or things found elsewhere in the universe.
Earthy has connotations of being close to the soil; thus, it pertains to things a bit low-down and dirty (or at least crude and uncultured).

By any earthly standard, Garg was not attractive.

Jessup stopped dating the princess when he discovered the more earthy attractions of the farmer's daughter.

GENDER DISORIENTATION II

43

Frances and *Francis* sound exactly alike, but females usually end it with an "e," males with an "i." Memory aid: Remember that Frances is a short form of Francesca.

GEOGRAPHICA CONFUSICA II

The old fishing and tourist town on the coast of California is *Monterey*. The city in northeastern Mexico is *Monterrey*.
Memory aid: To remember there are two "r's" in the Mexican municipality, keep in mind that Monterrey isn't far from Vera Cruz.

Emigrate/Immigrate

Emigrate: to leave one place (usually one's native land) to set up residence in another.
Immigrate: to come into a new place (usually a country) to set up residence.

> She could no longer cope with the rat race in the United States, so she emigrated to New Zealand, where she lived for the rest of her life.
> The United States is so large and varied that those who immigrate here can usually find a region with climate and topography similar to the ones they left behind.

MEMORY AID: Remember that to **emi**grate is to **em**bark.

Eminent/Imminent

Eminent (usually used to describe a person) means distinguished, outstanding, notable.
Imminent (usually used to describe an event) means close at hand, approaching, just about to happen.

> From the look of the craft, we were certain that it had brought someone or something of eminent rank.
> A door in the side opened, and we felt certain that an important meeting was imminent.

MEMORY AID: Think of **imm**inent and **imm**ediate.

Empathy/Sympathy

<u>Empathy</u> is "getting inside" another person or situation; identifying closely with someone else's feelings or experiences.

<u>Sympathy</u> is understanding another person's feelings or emotions.

Morgan had such empathy with the role he was portraying onstage that he began to act like the character twenty-four hours a day.

I have great sympathy for his wife, who must put up with his murderous rages.

MEMORY AID: In **empathy**, one's feelings resemble another's.

PERENNIAL SLIPUPS II

Its and *it's*. *Its*—without an apostrophe—is the possessive form of "it," indicating ownership or belonging to. (As in: Each word has its own meaning.) *It's*—with the apostrophe—is the contraction of "it is" or "it has." (As in: It's easy to mix up words.) Memory aid: Remember that "it's" usually does the same job as its cousin, "'tis."

Entomology/Etymology

<u>Entomology</u> is the study of insects.

<u>Etymology</u> is the study of words; specifically, the study of a particular word's history—tracing it back to its origins. (Etymology is also the name for the branch of linguistics that deals with such studies.)

This would be a great spot if you were interested in entomology, but it's a bad place for a picnic.

Knowing the etymology of a word often makes it easier to remember its meaning.

MEMORY AID: Since ants are insects, think of "antomology."

46

Epigram/Epigraph

An epigram is a terse, witty poem or saying.
An epigraph is an inscription on a building, or an introductory line or two at the opening of a book or the sections of a book. (Epigrams are often used as epigraphs.)

"Beautiful she is not; untalented, yes" is a favorite epigram of mine.
The epigraph at the beginning of the novel's second half set the stage for what was to come.

MEMORY AID: Epigrams are terse, like telegrams. Since epigraphs are associated with books, think of epigraph and paragraph.

Epitaph/Epithet

Epitaph: words inscribed on a tombstone.
Epithet: word or phrase used to characterize or describe a person or thing; it is not necessarily a negative description.

The name of the airline on the smoking wreckage seemed like an epitaph.
"The fabulous invalid" is an epithet often used to refer to the theater business in New York City.

MEMORY AID: The mournful notes of taps are sometimes played at funerals, so think if "epitaps." Remember that an epithet is often pithy.

Equable/Equitable

Equable means steady, even.
Equitable means fair and square, evenhanded.

The varied landscape, the pungent cooking, and the equable climate are only some of the things that I like about the south of France. Our local street gang has never been known as an equitable organization.

MEMORY AID: Remember that to lay your cards on the (equi) table is to be fair and aboveboard.

Equinox/Solstice

48

Each of these mileposts along the ceaseless swings of the sun occurs twice a year.

The vernal equinox (about March 22) occurs when the sun crosses the equator on its way north; the autumnal equinox (about September 22) is the moment Sol crosses the equator on his way south. The beginning of spring and fall, respectively; on both days there is an equal amount of light and darkness everywhere on the Earth.

The summer solstice (about June 22) occurs when the sun reaches its farthest point north; its farthest point south is the winter solstice (about December 22). The solstices are the longest and shortest days of the year and mark the beginning of summer and winter, respectively.

> Just like ancient peoples, we today observe major religious festivals at the times of the winter solstice and the vernal equinox.

MEMORY AID: **Equinox: equal** days.
Solstice: short and **long** days.

Evoke/Invoke

These get mixed up because both involve using something, or calling up something.
Evoke means to summon up or recreate something in the imagination.
Invoke means to call upon or refer to an authority—a law, for instance—for assistance or protection.

> The odor of creosote always evokes a particularly melancholy moment of my childhood.
> My older brother is always trying to invoke his rights as the firstborn.

49

MEMORY AID: Think of **e**voking **fe**elings.
Think of **in**voke as having elements of **inter**ference.

COLLECTIBLE CONUNDRUM

A *numismatist* is a collector of coins. A *philatelist* is a collector of stamps. Memory aid: Remember that the *p*hilatelist goes to the *p*ost office.

Exalt/Exult

Perhaps the reason these often get confused is because they both suggest a great joy and elevated spirits.

To exalt (almost always a transitive verb) is to glorify; to raise high in esteem or power.

To exult (almost always an intransitive verb) is to be very happy about something.

In these days of unrestrained mediocrity, we don't often get a chance to exalt a hero.

We often find it necessary to exult over small victories.

MEMORY AID: Think of exalt and altitude; exult and exuberant.

Faint/Feint

As an adjective, faint means indistinct or dim; as a verb, it means to swoon.

Feint means to fake an attack at one spot so as to more easily attack at another.

Seeing Claudia collapse yet again, I began to think that she liked to faint.

It could have been simply a feint to keep me from noticing that the real onslaught was about to unfold.

MEMORY AID: Think of faint and pain; feint and deceive.

Farther/Further

One has grown accustomed to hearing and seeing these two used interchangeably and indiscriminately, but to be precise, use farther only for physical distance, further for "greater extent"—as in "further discussion," "looking into matters further," and so on.

The farther we drove, the more I grew to loathe that monstrous landscape.
It was not long before I realized that we would not help our cause further in this dreadful place.

Faun/Fawn

A faun is the satyrlike woodland deity who is half man, half goat.
A fawn is a young deer; to fawn is to shower with affection and attention in a sickening, obsequious manner.

Always fantasizing about sex, Roger seemed a natural for the faun costume.
Ever the cynic, Dominic reminded us that the helpless-looking fawn would grow up to be an animal capable of devouring an entire vegetable garden in one night.

MEMORY AID: A faun is unreal.
To fawn is to say "aw" a lot.

GENDER DISORIENTATION III

Which is the female name, which the male—*Beverley* or *Beverly*? Although one meets more male "Bevs" in England than in the U.S., remember that the masculine spelling usually has the extra "e."

Ferment/Foment

Both have to do with agitation and change, but:
Ferment, both as a noun and an intransitive verb, indicates a state of unrest.
Foment, a transitive verb, means to instigate change, to stir people up.

The ferment on campus was due to the administration's new policy regarding a certain fermented beverage.

In an attempt to foment further trouble, some students passed out leaflets and made inflammatory speeches—others simply passed out.

MEMORY AID: A moment of foment.
An eternity of ferment.

Fewer/Less

Fewer ("not so many") deals with numbers of things. Less ("not so much of") deals with amounts. One hears "less" misused more often than "fewer." The phrases "less calories," "less innings," and "less books" are not good English.

At least there were now fewer moving things on top of the cake.
I was glad that I had used less butter than usual.

MEMORY AID: Fewer = number.
Less = mass.

Flair/Flare

A <u>flair</u> is an intrinsic talent or aptitude.
A <u>flare</u> is a sudden outburst—as of a flame, or anger.
It is also a shape that is wider at one end than at the other.

Even as a child, Monica Morris, D.D.S., had a flair for pulling teeth.
In the darkness of her office the flare of the struck match looked enormous.

Flaunt/Flout

Not only do these two sound similar, but there is a
touch of arrogance about both.
To <u>flaunt</u> is to show off in a flashy way.
To <u>flout</u> is to scornfully defy, to mock.

From what she did on top of the table, it was
obvious she had a deep need to flaunt her talent.
If she continues to flout the house rules, we
shall ask that she leave.

MEMORY AID: When one fl**outs**, one is a bit **outs**ide the
law (or at least outside convention).

Fleshly/Fleshy

Fleshly has to do with "pursuits of the flesh"—often grossly sexual ones.
Plump vegetables, fruits, and people are fleshy.

With a purple Cadillac, the pimp flaunted the rewards of fleshly activities.
Many men seem often to prefer fleshy women to skinnier ones.

Flotsam/Jetsam

Technically, under maritime law and the rules of salvage, flotsam is ship's cargo that is lost at sea and remains floating (not washed ashore); jetsam is cargo that is jettisoned (to lighten a ship in an emergency, for instance) and sinks to the bottom. Used figuratively—and much more usefully—the phrase "flotsam and jetsam" is used as a high-class term for "junk."

The weathered deck chair hanging over the mantel like a piece of sculpture is a piece of flotsam Jack found when sailing off Martha's Vineyard.
Desperate for a raft, the shipwrecked sailors put the jetsam to good use.

MEMORY AID: The word flotsam, of course, has "float" in its roots.

Flounder/Founder

The common confusion here occurs when the words are used (as verbs, of course) in reference to ships and boats.

To <u>flounder</u> means to wallow about, to struggle.
To <u>founder</u> is to come apart completely; to sink.

The rusty old tub floundered through the monstrous waves, and I feared she would founder at any moment.

MEMORY AID: Remember that a vessel is still **floating** when it's **flo**undering.

Foreword/Forward

A foreword is a prefacelike section of a book, usually written by someone other than the author. Forward has to do with moving onward or being placed ahead; a forward is a player positioned at the front of his team.

A foreword written by a well-known person can help sell copies of a book.
The fortune in my cookie read: "You will go forward into the future."

MEMORY AID: Foreword: a **word** be**fore**.

Fortuitous/Fortunate

Fortuitous refers to something that happens strictly by chance; accidental.
Fortunate refers to good luck, auspicious occurrences.

It was entirely fortuitous that I was standing on the corner when the gun battle broke out. It was fortunate that I wasn't struck by a bullet.

GEOGRAPHICA CONFUSICA III

A schoolboy in a small midwestern town once asked his geography teacher what the difference is between the Rhine and the Rhône. The teacher replied that she didn't think it mattered, she'd seen it spelled both ways.

What she might more accurately have told her pupil is that while both these important European rivers do rise in the mountains of Switzerland, the Rhine flows north—mostly through Germany—to the North Sea; the Rhône flows south—mostly through France—to the Mediterranean.

Memory aid: On a map, the Rhône goes down.

Gaff/Gaffe

A gaff is a hook with a handle used for lifting fish.
A gaffe is a social blunder.

Jimmie Lou fell overboard trying to get the gaff into the angry catfish.
A terrible gaffe resulted from Bruce's not realizing that the man was the hostess's husband.

MEMORY AID: Since the French are very conscious of social refinements, mentally put an accent on the "e" and think of "gaffé."

59

Gibe/Jibe/Jive

To gibe is to mock or scorn; a gibe is a mocking or scornful comment.
To jibe means to conform to or agree with. (It also means to change direction when sailing.)
Jive is lively swing music or a double-talk-y way of speaking.

His resignation speech was for the most part polite, but he got in a gibe or two at the end.
It is always a pleasure to meet someone whose prejudices jibe with mine.
You might say that graffiti is visual jive.

GEOGRAPHICA CONFUSICA IV

Guadalupe is the name of several places—including a river, an island, and two counties in the southeastern U.S. and Mexico. *Guadeloupe* is the French island in the West Indies. Memory aid: To remember that there is an "e" and an "o" in the island's name, think of Guad*elo*upe as being a good place to which to *elo*pe.

Gourmand/Gourmet

Both are folks who care a lot about food, but they care in quite different ways.
The gourmand is the one sitting at the table, napkin tucked under chin, knife and fork at the ready. He may or may not know much about food; his main concern is that there be a lot of it.

A <u>gourmet</u> is a discriminating person who cares a great deal about the subtlety and sensitivity with which dishes are prepared and meals are served. Properly, both words are nouns, but the universal adjectival use of "gourmet"—in describing any slightly pretentious meal, cook, or restaurant—has poached most of the flavor out of this once elegant word.

Like the gourmand that he is, Gilbert wolfed down a dozen oysters, a plate of pasta, two porterhouse steaks, an order of French fries, and then asked for a banana split.

I was unable to tell what made the sauce so special, but Theophile—a true gourmet—said that he detected a hint of saffron.

MEMORY AID: The gourm**and** says, "**And** I'll have that **and** that **and** that."

The gour**met** asks, "**May** I have a bit of that, please?"   **61**

Grill/Grille

These are both metal gratings, but:
Without the "e," a <u>grill</u> is what you cook on—and what the police do to you with their questions.
A <u>grille</u> is a grating that serves as a barrier or a screen—the shield that ventilates and protects the engine of a car, for instance.

The little man tossed several disagreeable-looking pieces of fowl onto the charcoal grill.
Somehow, Myra managed to wriggle through the grille on the window.

Hail/Hale

<u>Hail</u>, as a verb, means to greet or call out; as a noun, it is icy precipitation.
<u>Hale</u> (often followed by "hearty") means healthy.

Knowing how to hail a taxi adroitly is a handy urban skill.
Sometimes when trying to find a taxi, it helps to be quite hale.

MEMORY AID: You might want to think of hail as **hard rain**.
Notice that h-a-l-e, slightly rearranged, is the first part of **hea**lthy.

Hardy/Hearty

While there is a sense of robust vigor about both of these, hardy means strength and endurance, often against adverse conditions; hearty means spirited, jovial, plentiful.

The hardy little group slept on, despite the screeching and spitting of the winged pigs in the branches overhead.
The townspeople gave their rescuers a hearty welcome.

63

Healthful/Healthy

Healthful means conducive to good health.
Healthy means in good health.

They say that it's not healthful to sit around in a wet bathing suit, but I do it all the time.
Despite all the sleep and exercise he gets, Vernon is not healthy.

MEMORY AID: Think of certain things—apples, vitamins, exercise—as **full** of health (health**ful**).

Historic/Historical

Historic means notable or famous in the sweep of history.

Historical means having to do with history, or else it refers to something that is demonstrated by the past.

The historic eighteenth-century house was used for many years by the local historical society.
It is a historical fact that Richard Nixon never slept in this house.

Hoard/Horde

64 A hoard is a collection or stash of something considered valuable; to hoard is to collect or stash same. A horde is a vast throng, usually people.

During World War II it was considered almost treasonous to hoard canned goods.
Waving torches, a horde of peasants clambered up toward the castle.

MEMORY AID: You might think of ho**ard** and l**ard**er, a storage space.

UNLIKELY BEDFELLOWS I

Calendar and *calender*. A calendar is a device that helps keep track of the days and months of the year. A *calender* is a rolling machine used in the manufacture of certain kinds of cloth and paper.

Honorarium/Stipend

An honorarium is a fee paid for a service for which there is no set or customary price.

A stipend is a fixed amount of money paid periodically, particularly the payments made as an adjunct to a scholarship, fellowship, etc.

Professor Wield supplements his salary from the university by giving lectures to civic groups and always collecting an honorarium.

Michael was given a dwelling, transportation, and a monthly stipend that allowed him to live on the local economy.

MEMORY AID: You can de**pend** on a sti**pend**.

65

Human/Humane

All too often the first of these has exactly the opposite meaning of the second.

Human means having to do with the well-known race that dominates the planet Earth.

Humane means compassionate, kind.

I accidentally dropped a piece of equipment and the robot glared at me. "I'm only human!" I screamed.

The humane thing would have been to shoot the injured animal.

MEMORY AID: Hum**ane** has something of the **sane** in it.

Hyperthermia/Hypothemia

Hyperthermia is a very high fever, usually artificially induced for medical purposes.
Hypothemia is a very low body temperature, usually brought on by exposure to cold weather.

The doctor brought on a state of hyperthermia in the patient.
The water in the pool was so cold that Aunt Ethel had to kick briskly to avoid hypothemia.

Imply/Infer

Imply means to suggest or to insinuate; to communicate indirectly.
Infer means to deduce or to surmise; to come to a conclusion based on what is observed.

The look on her face implied that she disapproved of his childish conduct.
From the look on your face I infer that she didn't like what he was doing.

MEMORY AID: Remember that you imply *to* someone; you infer *from* someone.

Incredible/Incredulous   **67**

These two bear a strong family resemblance and both work in the believability business, but they have different jobs.
Incredible means, literally, not credible; it's what something is when it's not believable.
Incredulous means unbelieving; it's what you are when you don't believe something.

It seemed incredible to me that she had seen pigeons at that altitude.
I was incredulous when she told me she had snared one of the birds and served it for dinner.

MEMORY AID: Remember that things are incredible, people are incredulous.

Indeterminable/Indeterminate

Each of these refers to something that cannot be determined, but with a difference.
Indeterminable means incapable of being precisely limited, decided upon, or known.
Indeterminate means indefinite or unsettled as to type, time, etc.; vague.

An indeterminable number of insects swarmed about the tent.
Unpleasant flowers of a strange, indeterminate variety lined the pathway.

MEMORY AID: Unknowable is a synonym of indeterminable.

68

Indict/Indite

Indict: to formally charge with a crime.
Indite: to put into written words; to compose.

Even after seeing a film of the incident, the grand jury refused to indict the killer.
He seated himself at the desk and began to indite a speech of gratitude.

MEMORY AID: Think of indite and write.

Ingenious/Ingenuous

Ingenious means very clever, imaginative.
Ingenuous means guileless, candid, trusting.

The endlessly ingenious burglars of our town
can break into anything or any place.
The ingenuous newcomers smiled and nodded
to the man walking out with the VCR.

MEMORY AID: Think of ingenious and genius.

Inter- /Intra-

Inter- is a prefix that indicates between, among.
Intra- is a prefix that indicates within.

We will circulate an interdepartmental memo
so everyone in the company will be apprised of
the news.
The other memo was meant to be strictly
intradepartmental, so we don't know how the
whole place found out about it.

MEMORY AID: Think of **inter**state highway.

Interment/Internment

70

Interment is the burial of a dead person.
Internment is the confinement of people, usually for
political reasons.

In her will, Harvina left strict instructions
that her interment take place precisely at the
stroke of midnight.
Barbed wire, watchtowers, and snarling dogs
are the apparatus of internment.

MEMORY AID: You might think of in**term**ent and
terminal, or that underground insect the **term**ite.

Lath/Lathe

Lath (short "a") is the word for the long thin strips of wood used in construction of buildings as a support for plaster.

A lathe (long "a") is a machine that can shape a piece of wood or metal by rotating it against a blade.

The old house was falling apart, and here and there the plaster had fallen away to reveal the lath beneath.

Sophie made the most amazing candelabrum with the lathe in her home workshop.

Latitude/Longitude

The lines that go around a globe parallel with the equator are lines of latitude.

Lines of longitude are the "vertical" ones that start and finish at the North and South Poles.

She has convinced herself that all her problems will be solved by moving to a warmer latitude.

The jet plane almost kept up with the sun as it sped across the longitudes toward California.

MEMORY AID: Since flat slabs would result if you sliced the Earth along the lines of latitude, you might think of them as "flatitudes."

Laudable/Laudatory

Laudable means worthy of praise.
Laudatory means giving praise.

The personoids provided many laudable services in the days following The Split.
They seemed pleased by the laudatory message sent by the Main Custodian.

MEMORY AID: Laudable simply means **able** to be **lauded**.

Leeward/Windward

Leeward means protected from the wind or sailing in the same direction the wind is blowing.
Windward means facing the wind or sailing into it.

The island's prevailing winds are from the east, so we chose the Sunset Inn, assuming it was on the leeward side.
Our course was windward, which slowed us considerably.

MEMORY AID: There's **less** wind on the **lee** side.

Liable/Likely

Liable has to do with negative or harmful results. Likely is concerned with expected or probable outcomes.

If we're not nice to it, it's liable to attack at any moment.
If we survive, we're likely to see some fascinating sights.

MEMORY AID: Think of liable and libel—both unpleasant.

Literary/Literate

Literary: having to do with books and literature.
Literate: able to read; cultured and educated.

Many people consider having a job in the literary world to be smart and sophisticated.
More than just another spy adventure, the movie turned out to be an intelligent and literate comedy as well.

MEMORY AID: Think of liter**ate** and educ**ate**.

Loath/Loathe

Loath is the adjective meaning not wanting to do something; reluctant.
Loathe is the verb meaning to have disgust or hatred for something or somebody.

Having been warned about the visitor, Homer was loath to open the door.
"I loathe anything that has even been in the same room with you," Susan hissed.

MEMORY AID: You might remember that the last four letters of lo**athe** are an anagram for **hate**.

Luxuriant/Luxurious

Luxuriant, usually used to describe growing things, means bountiful, lush, copious.
Luxurious means elegantly and expensively appointed; plush.

The luxuriant fur of the two monkeys drew everyone's attention.
The luxurious duplex was easily affordable on the pair's sitcom earnings.

MEMORY AID: Since luxurious often has to do with habitations and surroundings, think of "luxuri-house."

Mantel/Mantle

Mantel: the structure that frames a fireplace.
Mantle: a covering or casing.

It darted up one side of the mantel, then saun-tered brazenly across the top and slid down the other side.
She felt almost regal as the mantle of office was literally and figuratively draped across her shoulders.

MEMORY AID: One can usually strike an effective pose with one **el**bow on a mant**el**.

Masterful/Masterly

A "take-charge kind of guy" could be described as masterful.

The work of a highly skilled person might be said to be masterly.

Rhett Butler in *Gone With the Wind* remains one of the screen's most masterful characters. Scarlett O'Hara was masterly at the art of getting what she wanted.

IN THE BEGINNING . . .

An *embryo* is a developing animal in its first stages; humans are embryos for two months after conception. A *fetus* exists in the later stages of development; in humans this runs from the end of the second month until birth. Memory aid: In the alphabet, as in nature, embryo comes before fetus.

Material/Matériel

Material, as a noun meaning substances or things, should not be used to refer to things military.

The word for weapons, vehicles, and other equipment and supplies of war is matériel.

Birds use a wide variety of material in nest-building.

Always a sucker for men in uniform, Frederica followed the convoy of army matériel down the highway.

MEMORY AID: Remember matériel and "war is hell."

Meddle/Metal/Mettle

To <u>meddle</u> is to butt into someone else's affairs.
<u>Metal</u> is a hard substance—iron, aluminum, etc.
<u>Mettle</u> is courage or stamina.

The words "I don't want to meddle, but . . ." usually mean that the speaker is just about to do just that.

I tested the metal, and it was pure 24-karat gold.

It took all my mettle to smile and nod through an hour's worth of free advice.

MEMORY AID: The most common error here is to use "metal" in the sense of showing or trying one's hardiness, so remember that to show your mettle, you should be in pretty good fettle.

Meteor/Meteorite

A <u>meteor</u> is a rocky object from outer space that burns up in Earth's atmosphere, and is visible as a quick, fiery streak across the night sky. When such an extraterrestrial visitor actually lands, as it occasionally does, it instantly becomes a <u>meteorite</u>.

People living in brightly lighted cities rarely see meteors.
Museums are about the only places where you can see meteorites.

MEMORY AID: As in meteorite, the suffix "ite" is found at the ends of many words for tangible substances— dynamite, cellulite, Kryptonite.

Moat/Mote

A moat is the protective trench around a castle or other building; it is usually filled with water.
A mote is a tiny particle.

Early each morning the king and queen practiced intricate swimming strokes in the moat.
A mote blew into my eye just as I was getting a good view.

MEMORY AID: You can float your boat in a moat.

Nauseated/Nauseous

Nauseated is the participle used to describe how you feel when you are sick to your stomach.
Nauseous is the adjective used to describe something that makes you feel sick to your stomach. No matter how many times friends tell you they are nauseous, they aren't—unless perhaps they haven't bathed for several weeks.

I grew quite nauseated as we sailed across the choppy sea toward the ancient port.
The open sewers created an overwhelmingly nauseous smell.

MEMORY AID: Think of nauseous as being close to noxious—as in "noxious fumes."

COLLEGE DAZE

An *alumna* (pl., *alumnae*) is a female graduate. A male grad is an *alumnus* (pl. *alumni*).

Negligent/Negligible

Negligent means careless, neglectful—particularly when the result may be harmful.
Negligible means trifling, unimportant (referring to the amount of something).

Knocking the highball off the edge of the balcony is only one example of his negligent behavior.
Luckily, the damage was negligible.

MEMORY AID: A **gent**leman is seldom negli**gent**.

Obelisk/Odalisque

A pillar with a pyramid-shaped top is an <u>obelisk</u>. An <u>odalisque</u>, once a female inhabitant of a Turkish harem, is now seen only in paintings, usually reclining on her side in a sultry pose.

We went all the way up to the top of the Washington Monument, the best-known obelisk in the U.S.

The odalisque, demurely holding a fan, stared haughtily down from the canvas.

MEMORY AID: **Ob**elisks are **ob**long. "Odal**isques**" are slightly **risqué**.

Official/Officious

Official, as an adjective, means real, authentic, authorized.

Officious, only an adjective, means meddlesome, intrusive; to act in an official way when not wanted or needed.

The official report was quite different from the rumors we had heard.

He jumped out into the street, blowing a whistle and directing traffic in an officious manner.

MEMORY AID: Besides officious, many "icious" words have negative connotations—capricious, factitious, malicious, pernicious, seditious, suspicious, avaricious, inauspicious, meretricious, surreptitious, vicious . . .

83

NO "S" IN U.S.

In America, *toward,* not *towards,* is the preferred form of the preposition meaning "in the direction of." In Britain, they tack on the final sibilant. *Backward, forward, downward, upward,* and *way* are also usually better off without the "s."

Ordinance/Ordnance

An <u>ordinance</u> is a law.
<u>Ordnance</u> is military supplies, particularly heavy weapons and ammunition.

Many people still observe the city ordinance that says vehicles must stop at red lights.
The Veterans Day parade included a lot of ordnance, which seemed to please the onlookers.

Palate/Palette/Pallet

<u>Palate</u>: the roof of the mouth; the sense of taste.
<u>Palette</u>: a board on which an artist mixes paints.
<u>Pallet</u>: a crude, makeshift bed.

His palate balked at the taste of armadillo for breakfast.
To paint the western sunset, he squeezed large amounts of red, yellow, and ocher onto his palette.
That night, even the pallet on the floor of the barn seemed comfortable.

MEMORY AID: **My palate ate.**
My little **pal** (**palette**) was full of paint.
My pall**et let** me sleep.

Pastiche/Postiche

A <u>pastiche</u> is a literary or musical work made up of bits and pieces of other works, or of a variety of styles. A <u>postiche</u> is a toupee.

The composer blended into a charming pastiche everything from early hoedown to late "get-down" music.

As he vigorously pounded the keys, his postiche flew from his head into a lap in the front row.

MEMORY AID: Think of a **pas**tiche as being **pas**ted together. (Indeed, it comes from **pas**ticcio, Italian for **pas**ty.)

Pendant/Pendent

A <u>pendant</u> is something suspended or hanging, such as a piece of jewelry or other ornament.
<u>Pendent</u> is an adjective meaning hanging or overhanging.

A huge diamond pendant hung from the necklace Isolda was wearing.
After a hundred thousand years the pendent rock formation came crashing down just at that moment.

MEMORY AID: Pen**dants dang**le.

Perquisite/Prerequisite

Perquisite: A special advantage or benefit of a job beyond the regular salary.
Prerequisite: Something necessary beforehand; something needed as a preparation for something else.

One of the perquisites of Henrietta's new role as leading lady was a twenty-four-hour-a-day limousine.
U.S. citizenship is one of the prerequisites for the job of president.

MEMORY AID: Remember that the slang word for perquisite is "perk."

Pore/Pour

To pore over is to look at or read very carefully. As a noun, a pore is a minute opening on the skin.
To pour is to cause something to flow from one place to another.

I watched the old woman pore over the crystal globe as though her life depended on it.
"I had better pour the tea," she said softly.

MEMORY AID: Think of poring over a person's face so closely that you can see each pore.

Poser/Poseur

A <u>poser</u> is someone who poses (as for a photograph); a difficult question or problem is also a poser.
A <u>poseur</u> is someone who takes on an identity not his own, or who behaves in an artificial, insincere manner.

It was a real poser trying to decide what to do with the information that it was my sister who had committed the crime.

The once-aristocratic spa now attracts only
phonies and parvenu poseurs.

MEMORY AID: Remember that the word poseur sounds
a bit fancied up and fake, just like what it means.

Practicable/Practical

These no-nonsense adjectives are near synonyms, but
there is a nice difference.
Practicable means feasible, possible to do or accomplish.
Things practical are also possible to do or accomplish,
but the word denotes sensibleness, usefulness, prag-
matism. (It also means virtual, in the sense of "to all
intents and purposes.")

It might be practicable to build a mousetrap in
which the rodent would be killed by gamma
rays, but the contraption wouldn't be practical
for general household use.

MEMORY AID: Practicable means **able** to be put into
practice.

THE BIBLE TELLS US SO

Perhaps because so many books of the Bible are plural
(Proverbs, Ecclesiastes, Lamentations, Ephesians, Ro-
mans, among others), many people write or say *Reve-
lations* when referring to the last book of the New
Testament. Actually, it is singular.

Premier/Premiere

As an adjective, <u>premier</u> refers to the first in time or the most important; as a noun, it means prime minister. As a noun, <u>premiere</u> means first public performance.

Her premier objective in going to the theater is to be seen in public.
Anyone who is anyone was at the premiere, each dressed to the nines.

Prescribe/Proscribe

Prescribe means to order, to direct; to write medical instructions.
Proscribe means to outlaw, to forbid.

I had hoped the doctor would prescribe a vacation instead of more of these odious little pills. If I had my way, I would proscribe much of the public behavior one sees today.

MEMORY AID: Think of **pro**scribe and **pro**hibit.

PERENNIAL SLIPUPS III

Port and *starboard*. The first thing to remember here is that these nautical terms apply when one is facing the bow of a boat or ship. When one is so facing, the *port* side is the left, *starboard* the right side. Memory aid: Remember that "port" and "left" each have the same number of letters.

Presumptive/Presumptuous

Presumptive pertains to something that one takes to be true based on a reasonable belief; it is most often a legal term.

Presumptuous means to presume too much, to overstep the bounds of propriety and therefore to appear arrogant and overbearing.

He was the only person found anywhere near the scene of the crime, but the evidence was only presumptive.

The jury didn't like the presumptuous attitude of the lawyer.

Principal/Principle

As a noun, principal is the person in the position of highest authority in an organization; it is also invested money. As an adjective, principal means main or primary.

Principle, a noun only, refers to a guiding doctrine or an underlying scientific law.

Miss Hyland, the principal, did not wish to retire, as she could not maintain her standard of living by living off her principal.

Most people understand the basic principle by which a violin works, but that doesn't mean they could construct one.

MEMORY AID: To remember that principal is a person, think of the principal as your pal.

To remember that principal is money, think of it as capital, or maybe alimony.

Remember that principle is never a person, and think of principle and rule.

Prophecy/Prophesy

Both of these involve foretelling the future, but one is a noun, the other a verb.

Prophecy (final syllable pronounced "see") is the noun, meaning a prediction.

Prophesy (final syllable pronounced "sigh") is the verb, meaning to predict.

The woman claimed she'd never been wrong about a prophecy, but we couldn't believe what she told us would come true.

Politicians love to prophesy about the economic future of the country.

Rack/Wrack

There's usually no problem remembering to use rack—not wrack—when referring to the scoring or amassing of points. The trouble may come when talking about instances of great stress. The correct choice in those cases is rack. The rack was a medieval instrument of torture upon which the victim was actually stretched; ergo, to rack is to subject to strain. Wrack comes from "wreck," and means to do just that—but completely.

The pounding waves continued to rack the hapless vessel, but it survived the storm.
The storm moved on to wrack the seaside cottage, reducing it to rubble.

MEMORY AID: To rack is, figuratively, to put on the rack.

Ravage/Ravish

While both of these involve violence and destruction, to ravage is to wreak havoc generally; to ravish is to take by force, to rape.

We sat sipping iced tea as the termites continued to ravage the very floorboards beneath us.
The winged pigs, now totally mad, continued to ravish the villagers.

Rebound/Redound

These both have an element of something coming back toward one.

<u>Rebound</u> means to bounce back or ricochet.

<u>Redound</u> (usually followed by "to" or "upon") refers to the effect—good or bad—that an action will have, often in the sense of "coming home to roost."

Myron caught the ball on the rebound.
The team's success—or lack of it—will always redound upon the coach.

MEMORY AID: Remember that **redo**und will figuratively **redo** itself.

Regime/Regimen

A regime is a form or system of government.
A regimen is also a kind of system, but it's used in the sense of a routine.
The common confusion is to use regime for the "routine" sense.

Since Katya grew up under a totalitarian regime, she found it hard to adjust to the hurly-burly society of the U.S.
There were some unusual exercises in the daily regimen my doctor prescribed.

MEMORY AID: **Regimen** is **regimen**ted behavior.

Reign/Rein

Reign can be both verb and noun, and pertains to what a monarch does when he or she rules; it thus means to dominate or to prevail.
Rein, as a noun, is a restraint or a curb; as a verb it means to restrain or to curb.

On the day of complete gridlock in Manhattan, pandemonium will reign.
Cabdrivers in particular give free rein to individual expression.

MEMORY AID: Think of a sove**reign reign**ing.
Think of **rein**ing in a **rein**deer.

Review/Revue

A review is a critical appraisal of a book, movie, theater performance, etc.
A revue is a lighthearted theatrical presentation, usually made up of short segments, often containing topical material.

"I hate the theater," said the drama critic. "I never go. Friends call me up and tell me about it and then I write my review."
One skit in the revue portrayed the mayor as a clog-dancing crocodile.

MEMORY AID: Remember that a re**view** is a **view**point. Remember that **cue** is a theater word, just as is rev**ue.**

Rout/Route

Part of the confusion here probably stems from pronunciation problems; both of these are often pronounced alike, but route—properly—rhymes with scoot; rout rhymes with scout.

To <u>rout</u> means to kick out, or to defeat overwhelmingly. Rout is also a noun that means a terrible defeat or a disorderly retreat.

A <u>route</u> is the way you get from one place to another.

Tenacious as they were, I finally managed to rout them from under my sink.

Cathy wasn't much of a trip planner; the arrow-straight route she discovered turned out to be a crease in the map.

MEMORY AID: When I say rout
I mean get out!
I repeat the route
On my daily commute.

Sanatorium/Sanitarium

Older dictionaries define <u>sanatorium</u> as an institution for the care of victims of tuberculosis, and <u>sanitarium</u> as an institution for the care of the insane. Both words are now a bit old-fashioned, but when they do come up, sanatorium usually means a spa or health resort, sanitarium a hospital of any kind.

Edwina spent most of her vacation at a sanatorium in the Alps.

We finally had no choice but to take Everett to a sanitarium.

MEMORY AID: Think of sana**tor**ium and **resort**.

Scare/Scarify

Scare means to frighten.
Scarify means to lacerate—particularly the skin or
the feelings of another person. (Scarify does not mean
to scare, no matter how many times or in what high
places you see it used in that sense.)

Even the wildest masks could not scare Baby
John.
The doctor had to scarify John's leg before
inoculating him.

MEMORY AID: Even though the "a" in scarify is
pronounced almost the same as in scare, think of
scarify as meaning "to scar."

Scrip/Script

Scrip is currency issued in special situations, or a small certificate indicating payment due.
Script is handwriting or the written text of a play, movie, etc.

The occupying forces were paid in scrip, usable only in military stores, clubs, etc.
Henrietta decided to abandon the hateful script altogether and simply ad-lib her way through the rest of the play

---

MEMORY AID: Since scrip is usually small pieces of paper, think of scrip and scrap.

100

Seasonable/Seasonal

Seasonable means right and proper for the season of the year, or for the time.
Seasonal means affected by or changing with the seasons.

The room was well heated against the November chill, but shorts and sandals were not seasonable attire.
There were hardly any other guests in the hotel, as this a seasonal resort.

MEMORY AID: Think of seasonable and reasonable.

Sensual/Sensuous

Both partners of this closely linked adjectival couple
refer to things that appeal to the senses, but:
Sensual has implications of physical gratification.
Sensuous applies to "higher" or more aesthetic matters.

There were other sensual pleasures in store for
us that afternoon—lobster quiche and cham-
pagne.
The fleecy clouds overhead formed sensuous
patterns in the azure sky.

MEMORY AID: Think of sensual and sexual.

Shear/Sheer/Shirr

Perhaps one of the confusing things here is the association with fabric in one of the meanings of each word.

The principal meaning of shear is to cut or to clip; shears are scissors.

Sheer, an adjective, has several meanings: It refers to surfaces that are very steep; things that are pure and unalloyed; things that are thin and diaphanous.

To shirr (rhymes with her) is to gather fabric by pulling on certain threads. It's also a way to cook eggs.

Once a year they shear the llamas.
It was a sheer drop from the ledge to the water below.
Cora doesn't know how to boil an egg, much less shirr one.

MEMORY AID: Since the action of tearing apart is somewhat like shearing, think of shear and tear. Think of steep and sheer; and remember that you can peer through something sheer.

Simple/Simplistic

Simple means uncomplicated, straightforward.
Simplistic is a derogatory term—usually used in reference to concepts and ideas—that means oversimplified and blind to complexities.

Fast-food restaurants have very simple menus.
To think of all international problems as a struggle between capitalism and communism is a simplistic world view.

Solecism/Solipsism

A solecism is a mistake in grammar or a small blooper in speech.
Solipsism is a philosophical theory that says that the only existent thing is the self.

Confusion Reigns is the kind of book that should contain no solecisms.
The "me" generation practiced a kind of pop version of solipsism.

MEMORY AID: Soloi was an ancient town where ungrammatical Greek was spoken, so the word solecism comes originally from "Soloi-ism." You might want to think of **sole**cisms being spoken in modern-day **Seoul** ("Seoulicisms").
To remember that solipsism is a philosophy, think of **pilop**sism."

103

GEOGRAPHICA CONFUSICA V

Three thousand miles separate *Stamford*, Connecticut, and *Stanford* University in Stanford, California, but how to remember which one has the "m" and which one the "n"? Memory aid: Remember that Sta*n*ford is near Sa*n* Francisco.

Solid/Stolid

Solid means without breaks or openings; firm, sturdy, reliable.

Stolid is usually used in reference to people, and it means having little or no emotion; impassive, dull.

"I'm looking for a good, solid 'yes' or 'no'—no more 'definite maybes,'" Jordan announced.
People of northern countries generally appear to be more stolid than those from more southern climates.

MEMORY AID: Think of **stolid** and **stoic**.

104

Stage Left/Stage Right

As an actor faces the audience, his or her left is stage left.

Stage right is on the actor's right side.

Forgetting what they had rehearsed, Mr. Toggle marched resolutely stage left shouting, "To war!"
Meanwhile, the sounds of raging battle came distinctly from stage right.

MEMORY AID: If, as William Shakespeare said, "All the world's a stage," then left and right are the same onstage as they are everywhere else.

Stalactite/Stalagmite

With the "ctite," it is a calcareous deposit hanging down from the roof of a cave.
With the "gmite," it is such a deposit rising up from the cave's floor.

The bats dodged among the stalactites like crazed toy airplanes.
The misshapen stalagmite rising before us reminded me of someone I knew.

Stationary/Stationery

Stationary is when things are immobile; firmly placed in one spot.
Stationery is what you write on.

The desk was built into the bookcase, and was absolutely stationary.
I sat down, chose some blue stationery, and began penning a letter.

MEMORY AID: Stationery is paper.

Stentorian/Stertorous

106   Stentor was an ancient Greek with an uncommonly powerful voice, and from that source comes stentorian, meaning very loud.
Stertorous, which is onomatopoeic, describes a harsh, raspy snoring sound.

Our next-door neighbors have such stentorian voices that we can hear every word they say.
From the stertorous sounds coming from the bedroom, we were certain that Uncle Stuart was sound asleep.

MEMORY AID: Since we all know how much noise most of them make, think of senators and stentors.

Through/Until

These two get confused mainly when referring to the limits of a specific period of time. Through, in this sense, means up to and including; until means only up to.

Mr. Rodgers will be here in the office through March 6; that is, he will be here until March 7.

MEMORY AID: Think of through and throughout.

Tocsin/Toxin

A tocsin is a bell used as an alarm signal.
A toxin is an animal- or vegetable-based poison.

At the clang of the tocsin the volunteers raced through the old streets toward the firehouse. The toxin in the pork worked fast, and Hildegarde was soon face down in her lo mein.

MEMORY AID: Think of the "x" in toxin as the crossed bones of the skull-and-crossbones poison symbol.

PERENNIAL SLIPUPS IV

Naval and *navel*. *Naval* is an adjective referring to things that have to do with a navy. *Navel* is a noun that refers to that spot on the human body where the umbilical cord was once attached. It's also the central point of something. Memory aid: Think of nav*el* and be*ll*ybutton; admira*l* and nav*al*.

Tortoise/Turtle

<u>Tortoise</u> is what you call a turtle that lives on land; it usually has a high domed shell and clublike feet that are adapted to walking.

<u>Turtle</u> is what you call a turtle that spends most of its life in or around water; it usually has a shell that is quite flat, and some species have webbed feet.

The tortoise trudged across the desert toward the dusty village.

Around and around the island swam the turtle.

Tortuous/Torturous

A tortuous road may make for torturous driving conditions; tortuous means twisted and sinuous, torturous means causing torturelike pains.

The only way up to the top was a tortuous maze of trails through the stunted gorse.
The doctor's treatment of my sprained ankle was a torturous experience.

MEMORY AID: A tortuous road might well be full of U-turns, so you might think of tortuous.
And, of course, torturous is close to torture.

Translate/Transliterate

To translate is to change words from one language into words of another language.
To transliterate is to change words from one alphabet into those of another alphabet.

The name of the capital of China translates as "Northern Peace."
The name of the capital of China used to be transliterated into the Roman alphabet as Peking; the modern transliteration is Beijing.

MEMORY AID: Think of transliterate misspelled as "transletterate," since it has to do with letters of the alphabet.

Translucent/Transparent

<u>Translucent</u> objects allow only light to pass through (e.g., a window with frosted glass).

<u>Transparent</u> objects are ones you can see through (e.g., a plain-glass window).

The pink bulbs, shining through the translucent plastic panels, gave the room a warm glow.

Allerton and Sybil were alarmed to discover that one wall of the room was completely transparent.

MEMORY AID: Trans**parent** has an element of ap**parent**.

Transsexual/Transvestite

A <u>transsexual</u> is a person who feels that he or she belongs physically to the wrong sex—sometimes to the point of having a sex-change operation.
A <u>transvestite</u> is a person (usually male) who for psychological reasons dresses in the clothes of the opposite sex.

"My body is a temple," said the transsexual. "I only wish it were more Diana and less Adonis."
I suddenly realized that the transvestite sitting demurely next to me at the bar was the man who delivers my mail.

MEMORY AID: Since *vestire* is Latin for "to clothe," transvestite literally means cross-dresser.

111

Troop/Troupe

As nouns, both are groups of people, but <u>troop</u> refers to military or quasi-military units and flocks of mammals or birds; as a verb, it means to move about in crowds.

<u>Troupe</u>, both as noun and verb, usually refers to theatrical performers.

A troop of apes swung unexpectedly into view. Each Saturday the family next door would troop off to a different shopping mall.

A troupe of jugglers and acrobats was also staying in our hotel.

MEMORY AID: Since actors often wear wigs, think of tr**oupe** and t**oupee**.

112

Tropic of Cancer/Tropic of Capricorn

These are the two imaginary lines that circle the Earth 23½ degrees north and south of the equator; they mark the northernmost and southernmost boundaries of the march of the sun. <u>Cancer</u> is the northern one, <u>Capricorn</u> the southern.

On our zigzag cruise of the Caribbean we crossed the Tropic of Cancer four times.
By far the largest land area that the Tropic of Capricorn crosses is Australia.

MEMORY AID: Since the Tropic of **Cancer** is the northern one, think of it as being the one closer to **Canada**.
Since Rio de Janeiro is almost on the Tropic of Capricorn, you might want to think of the "Cap**rio**corn."

113

Turbid/Turgid

These sound as though they should have similar meanings, but they are quite far apart. The meanings of both words are used literally and figuratively.
Turbid: stirred up so as to be murky, clouded, muddled.
Turgid: swollen, bloated, inflated, inflexible.

So many motorboats roar about the lake that the once-clear water is now quite turbid.
The Maltese Falcon is one of the rare movies in which the turbid plot gives the film its style.

MEMORY AID: Think of **turb**id and a **turb**ine, which stirs things up; think of tur**gid** and ri**gid**.

114

Unexceptionable/Unexceptional

Two letters make a world of difference here, for these two words are near opposites in meaning.
Unexceptionable means "beyond taking exception to"; in other words, something so nearly perfect that there are no exceptions or qualifications.
Unexceptional, a much more common word, means nothing exceptional, nothing out of the ordinary.

A gold medal at the Olympics is a reward for an unexceptionable performance.
Regrettably, Dan's workout on the parallel bars today was unexceptional.

Urban/Urbane

Urban: characteristic of a city.
Urbane: sophisticated, suave.

Born and raised in the country, Homer never really understood urban life.
With the help of a well-cut suit, an expensive tie, and a self-confident stride, Homer managed to project a convincingly urbane image.

Vale/Veil

Vale is a poetic word for valley. It is also used figuratively to refer to life on earth, as contrasted with the hereafter.
A veil is a thin, curtainlike covering or shield.

Even locked in winter's vise, the little vale has a serene, homey feeling.
I was fascinated by all the things she was able to do through the veil of that hat.

MEMORY AID: It's easy to remember that vale is valley, but it's harder to remember that the expression is *not* "veil of tears."

Venal/Venial

Venal means able to be bribed or corrupted.
Venial refers to an error that is minor enough to be pardoned or excused.

Organized crime exercises power by giving money to venal politicians.
Cutting down a cherry tree is a venial sin.

MEMORY AID: Those who practice
Action venal
May end up
In someplace penal.

Little sins,
The ones most trivial,
Are overlooked
As only venial.

Vertex/Vortex

A vertex is the highest point—of a building, hill, etc.; it is also the place, in many geometric figures, where two lines meet.
A vortex is the spinning center of a violent storm or turbulent section of water; a whirlpool.

Murray stood at the vertex of the pyramid and gazed down on the ancient land below.
The vortex of the storm passed directly across the structure, but did not disturb a single stone.

MEMORY AID: Think of the "o" in vortex as a tight, whirling circle of air or water.

Vice/Vise

Vice is depraved (or simply bad or unhealthful) conduct. It is also a prefix for titles of those second in
command. Pronounced with two syllables, it is a preposition that means "instead of," and as such appears
frequently with "versa."
A vise is a workshop tool that holds an object tightly
in one position.

In today's society it seems odd to think that
card-playing was once considered to be a
shameful vice.
The dog had the ace of hearts clenched in his
viselike jaws.

MEMORY AID: Playing with dice is a minor vice.
A vise is secure.

117

Want/Wont

Want is either a verb meaning to desire, to hanker
after, or a noun meaning scarcity, or lack of.
Wont is a noun meaning habit or practice. (With an
apostrophe, of course, "won't" is the contraction of
"will not.")

I love this store, and I want everything in it; I
know that seems selfish, considering all the
want in the world.
I paid cash, as is my wont.

Wiggle/Wriggle

A wiggle is a short, jerky, jiggly motion—toes, fingers, hips, and loose pieces of machinery wiggle—and there is often an element of fun in the word. A wriggle is more of a whole-body squirm; you don't wiggle through the hole in the fence, you wriggle through. Used figuratively, you wriggle out of a situation, but you "get a wiggle on" when you are in a hurry.

Haspel wiggled his foot just above the water, apparently trying to get the creature's attention.

An amorphous black shape wriggled out from beneath the rock and shot up toward the surface.

MEMORY AID: The **pig's** tail **wiggles**, the **wrestler wriggles**.

Wreak/Wreck

Wreak means to inflict or vent.
Wreck, of course, means to destroy. The confusion comes in misusing "wreck" in clichés like "wreak havoc."

The barrage prompted the defenders to wreak their vengeance on the invaders.
The ceaseless bombings continued to wreck our fortifications.

Yoke/Yolk

A yoke is any kind of restraint, particularly the wooden harnesslike contraption around the necks of a working pair of oxen.
An egg yolk is much more familiar.

The animals wheezed and snorted as they labored beneath the creaking yoke.
Reaching the limits of boredom, Pamela stabbed the cigarette out in the yolk of her half-eaten egg.

MEMORY AID: Some people associate **yoke**s with **yoke**ls and yolks with skillets.